CORE SKILLS

FIND IT:
SEARCHING FOR INFORMATION

Miriam Coleman

PowerKiDS
press
New York

Published in 2013 by The Rosen Publishing Group, Inc.
29 East 21st Street, New York, NY 10010

First Edition

Editor: Joanne Randolph
Book Design: Kate Laczynski

Photo Credits: Cover, p. 11 Jupiterimages/Comstock/Thinkstock; p. 4 Digital Vision/Photodisc/Thinkstock; pp. 5, 25 wavebreakmedia ltd/Shutterstock.com; p. 6 Maitree Laipitaksin/Shutterstock.com; p. 7 Fauvel/ The Bridgeman Art Library/Getty Images; p. 8 Stock Montage/Contributor/Archive Photos/Getty Images; p. 13 (top) Krzysztof Odziomek/Shutterstock.com; p. 13 (bottom) hkannn/Shutterstock.com; p. 15 photogl/ Shutterstock.com; p. 16 © iStockphoto.com/Hillary Fox; p. 20 (bottom) © iStockphoto.com/William Davies; p. 21 Barry Winiker/Photolibrary/Getty Images; p. 22 Lisa F. Young/Shutterstock.com; p. 23 LWA/Riser/ Getty Images; p. 24 © iStockphoto.com/Hanquan Chen; p. 26 iStockphoto/Thinkstock; p. 28 Fukuoka Irina/ Shutterstock.com; p. 29 S. Duffett/Shutterstock.com; p. 30 Jupiterimages/Photos.com/Thinkstock.

Library of Congress Cataloging-in-Publication Data

Coleman, Miriam.
 Find it : searching for information / by Miriam Coleman. — 1st ed.
    p. cm. — (Core skills)
 Includes index.
 ISBN 978-1-4488-7451-4 (library binding) — ISBN 978-1-4488-7536-8 (pbk.) —
 ISBN 978-1-4488-7598-6 (6-pack)
 1. Research—Methodology—Juvenile literature. 2. Information resources—Juvenile literature. I. Title.
 ZA3080.C65 2013
 001.4'2—dc23
                                              2012003846

Manufactured in the United States of America

CPSIA Compliance Information: Batch #SW12PK: For Further Information contact Rosen Publishing, New York, New York at 1-800-237-9932

Contents

WHAT IS INFORMATION?

Information is all around you. It can be found in books and newspapers and on websites if you know how to look for it. Information can even be found through your own scientific **observations**.

Information is the **foundation** of knowledge. If you want to learn about something, you search for

We get information about what is going on in the world around us from newspapers or watching the news. We can also find this information on the Internet.

In school, we get information from our teachers and from each other. A teacher uses books, lesson plans, and websites to research what she will share with a class.

information about it. Information is made up of facts and **details**. When you find out what kind of food an animal eats, this is information. Information answers the questions who, what, where, when, and how.

Information will provide the building blocks for any research project you do. How will you find the information, though? What will you do with what you find?

WHAT ARE YOU LOOKING FOR?

It is important to begin a project by thinking about what kind of information you need. What kind of project are you doing? What do you need to find out and what kind of sources will help you find the answers?

To do a report on animals of the forest biome, you would go to the library and look for books on the topic. You could also do an Internet search for "forest biome animals" and look for results that end in ".edu" or ".org."

For a project you are doing on the Battle of Saratoga, your Internet research might include a stop at the National Park Service site to download its student research packet on this battle.

If you are doing a report on one of the battles of the American Revolution, you will be looking for accounts of the battles, information about people who lived at that time, and maps of the area where the battle was fought. The information you seek might be found in history books and **almanacs** as well as diaries and letters written by people who lived at the time.

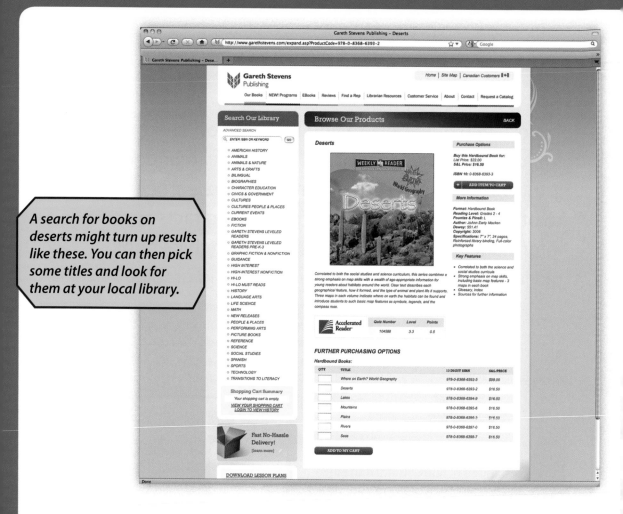

A search for books on deserts might turn up results like these. You can then pick some titles and look for them at your local library.

A good researcher knows that it takes several sources of information to learn about a subject. A single book or article is not enough to give a complete picture on a subject. Good research usually involves using several different types of sources as well. Research takes time and planning. Sometimes it takes creative thinking to find good sources, too.

HOW TO LOOK FOR PRINT SOURCES

If you are looking for print sources about your topic, a library catalog can tell you what sources are available and where to find them. You can search a library catalog by subject, keyword, author, or title.

> When looking for books, check the library catalog to find out where books on a topic are found. Then head there and start looking at the titles and indexes to find the ones that best suit your needs.

Books

Books are grouped together on library shelves based on subject. The library catalog will give you a call number for a book, which will tell you where the book can be found. If you are writing a report about sharks, you will find all the shark books together on the shelf. You might want to check out a large encyclopedia of sharks, a more specific book about whale sharks, or one about how sharks swim.

Online databases can be great sources for articles on your topic. If you see a box with an arrow in it, that means there is also a video to watch on your topic.

Life Cycle of a Praying Mantis

Next Section »

Listen

Hatching in Spring

In late spring, 50 to 400 **praying** mantises hatch from a single egg case. Each baby **mantis** is in a clear, thin sac that hangs from the egg case. The babies fight their way out of the sacs. Each one climbs a thread to the top of the egg case or onto a nearby branch. The **praying** mantises,

Praying mantises use camouflage to blend in with their surroundings.
© www.istockphoto.com/Morley Read

also called mantids, wait for a few hours as their soft, **transparent** skin darkens and hardens into a shell. The mantids may be eaten by lizards, spiders, frogs, ants, or even other mantids!

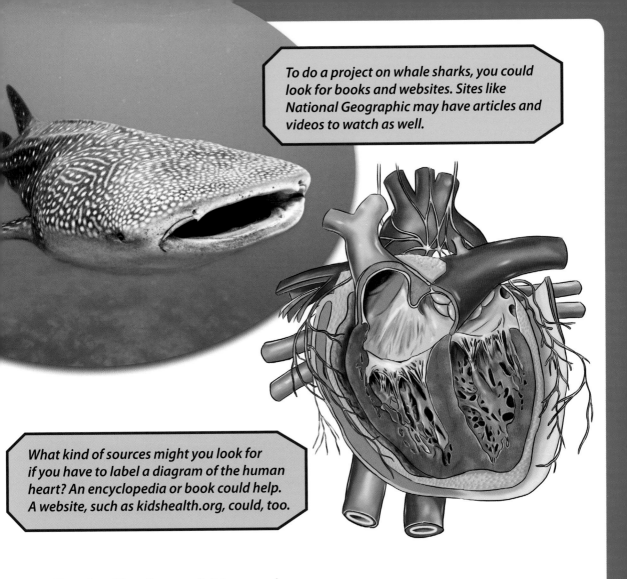

To do a project on whale sharks, you could look for books and websites. Sites like National Geographic may have articles and videos to watch as well.

What kind of sources might you look for if you have to label a diagram of the human heart? An encyclopedia or book could help. A website, such as kidshealth.org, could, too.

Periodicals and Magazines

Periodicals and magazines are great resources if you are looking for up-to-date information about current events or topics that change frequently. If you are doing a project about bedbugs, you might check a periodical or magazine to find out how many bedbug

Bibliography:

Bruhn, Dr. Aron. *Inside: Human Body*. New York: Sterling Publishing, 2010.

Johnson, Rebecca L. *Amazing DNA*. Minneapolis: Millbrook Press, 2008.

Johnson, Rebecca L. *Powerful Plant Cells*. Minneapolis: Millbrook Pres, 2008.

Walker, Richard. *Encyclopedia of the Human Body*. New York: DK Publishing, 2002.

Sandvold, Lynette Brent. *Genetics*. Tarrytown, NY: Marshall Cavendish Benchmark, 2010.

Winston, Robert. *Evolution Revolution: From Darwin to DNA*. New York: DK Publishing, 2009.

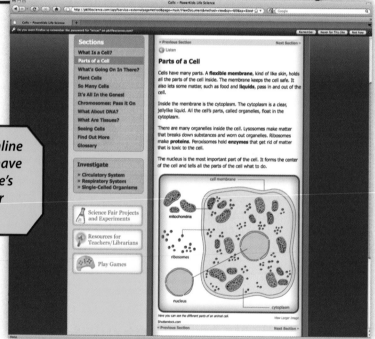

Let's say you find a great article online about cells. Your search does not have to stop there. Looking at the source's reference list can give you ideas for other places to look, too.

cases were reported in your state over the past year. Libraries often have both hard copies and electronic copies of periodicals and magazines, and many of these publications are also available on the Internet.

Other Print Materials

Firsthand accounts, or primary sources, offer more personal and immediate views of history. If you are working on a project about the Civil War, you might find letters or diaries written by soldiers to help you better understand what their lives were like.

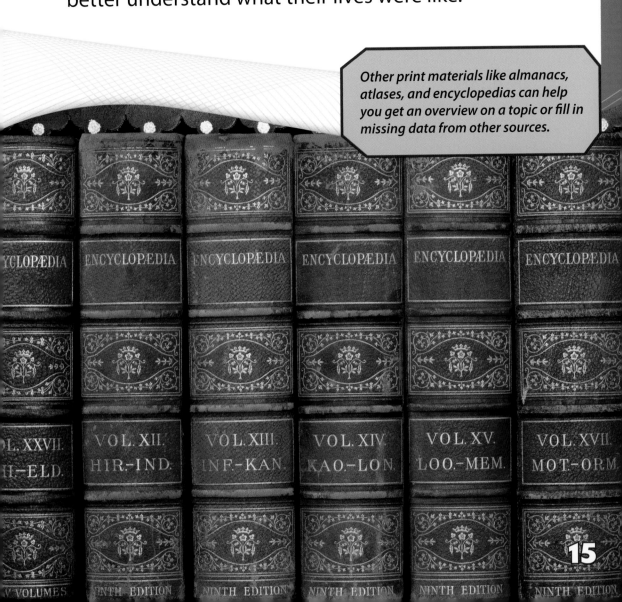

Other print materials like almanacs, atlases, and encyclopedias can help you get an overview on a topic or fill in missing data from other sources.

ENCYCLOPÆDIA | ENCYCLOPÆDIA | ENCYCLOPÆDIA | ENCYCLOPÆDIA | ENCYCLOPÆDIA | ENCYCLOPÆDIA

L. XXVII. | VOL. XII. | VOL. XIII. | VOL. XIV. | VOL. XV. | VOL. XVII.
HI.–ELD. | HIR.–IND. | INF.–KAN. | KAO.–LON. | LOO.–MEM. | MOT–ORM.

V VOLUMES | NINTH EDITION | NINTH EDITION | NINTH EDITION | NINTH EDITION | NINTH EDITION

HOW TO USE A SEARCH ENGINE

A search engine is a program that gathers information from millions of websites all over the Internet. Google and Yahoo are just two of the many free search engines that you can use to find huge amounts of information instantly.

> There are many different search engines. They will all pull up websites and other digital media based on the words you type into the search box.

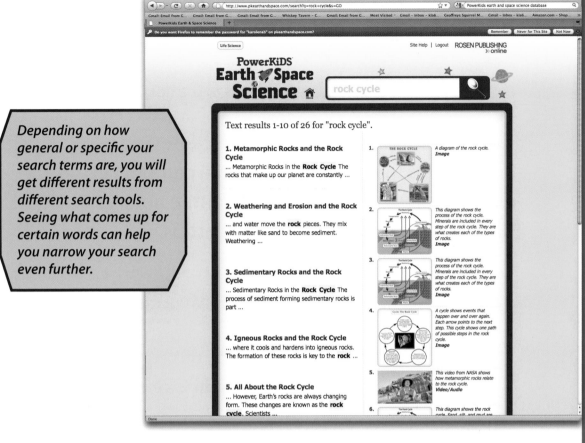

To use a search engine, you simply type keywords and phrases into the search field. The search engine will come up with a list of links to articles and websites that concern your topic. It is usually better to use specific words for your search so that you do not end up with too many results. If you want to search for a phrase, put it in quotation marks.

QUICK TIP

Many search engines let you narrow your search to find information in a specific format, such as electronic books, images, or maps.

WHAT ARE DIGITAL SOURCES?

Digital sources are an electronic form of information that you can read on a computer. Using digital sources, you can have an entire library's worth of information at your fingertips.

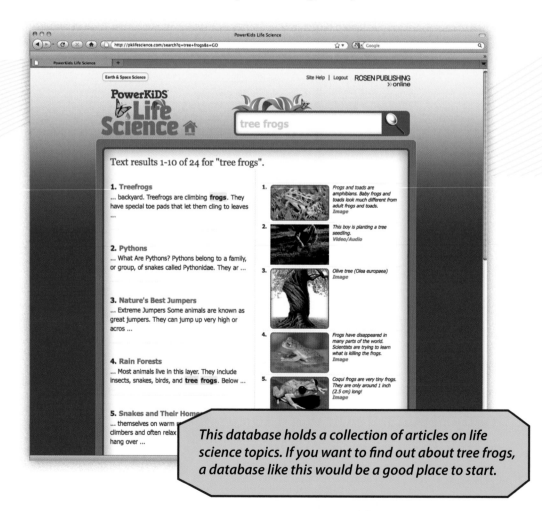

This database holds a collection of articles on life science topics. If you want to find out about tree frogs, a database like this would be a good place to start.

THE TWO PANDAS

Scientists have studied the giant panda and the red panda to figure out if the two **species** are related. They also want to know to which other animals they are related. Sorting animals in this way is called classification. Studies of the giant

Giant pandas look a lot like other bears. This gave scientists a clue as to where to start when classifying this panda.

People thought red pandas were related to raccoons because of the white masks on their faces and the rings on their tails.

panda's genetic code have led scientists to group this animal with the bear family.

Red pandas were once thought to be part of the raccoon family because their bodies looked similar to raccoons'. They were also once classified with the bear family. Scientists have since decided that red pandas do not have any close living relatives. Today they are in a family all by themselves!

8

9

E-books often have features that print books do not have. There may be buttons to click that bring up videos, extra pictures, or even games and quizzes.

Websites

There are thousands of websites on the Internet on almost any topic you can imagine. The websites of museums, educational **institutions**, and historic places can be great sources of information for school projects.

Online Databases

A database is a collection of information arranged in a way that makes it easy to find what you are looking for. A database can be a list of books, a set of links to other articles, or sets of **statistics**. You can **access** some databases anywhere, but others are available only at schools or libraries through a **subscription**.

E-Books

E-books are electronic books, which you can read on your computer or on a machine called an e-reader or a tablet. You can store hundreds of books on just one small device, and they take just seconds to **download**. You can also search the text of an e-book for words or phrases, which will help you find the information you need quickly.

What sources might you use to find out about the life cycle of lions? National Geographic's website could be one place to start. The library will have plenty of books on lions, too.

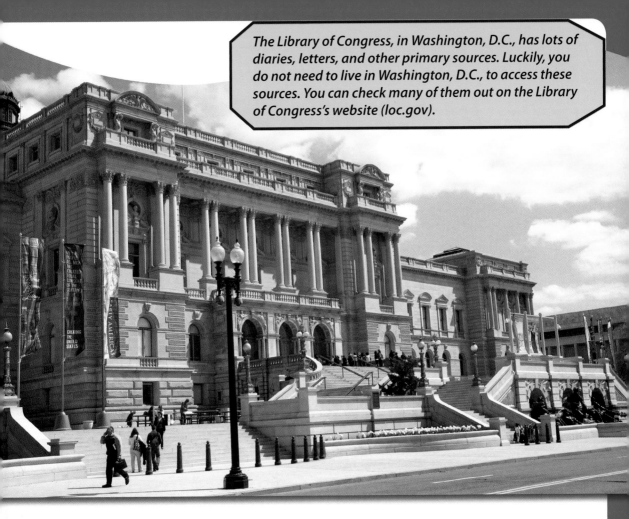

The Library of Congress, in Washington, D.C., has lots of diaries, letters, and other primary sources. Luckily, you do not need to live in Washington, D.C., to access these sources. You can check many of them out on the Library of Congress's website (loc.gov).

Video Sources

Watching videos can be fun, but you can also learn a lot from the right video sources. If you want to learn about wild animals, sometimes the best way is to see them in action, hunting, eating, or running through their natural habitats in a video. Watching a video about the American Revolution can help bring an important part of history to life.

HOW TO FIND THE BEST SOURCES

While conducting your research, you will probably come across a lot of sources that are not accurate. It is important to know how to tell which sources are reliable.

Pay attention to who wrote the information and when it was written. Was the author an expert in her field? Did the author cite sources? Websites and articles that are associated with universities or the government usually have addresses that end in .gov

If you are unsure about a source, ask your teacher or librarian to take a look at it.

A textbook is an example of a nonfiction book, or a book that has facts in it. Textbooks, encyclopedias, atlases, and nonfiction books can be good sources.

or .edu. These should be reliable. Even so, if a piece of information seems surprising or unlikely, you should confirm it by finding a second good source for the fact.

Beware of sources based on opinion rather than fact. Personal websites are rarely

QUICK TIP

As you find good sources, make note of them in a bibliography or reference list. This will help you find those sources again if you need them. This will also show that the facts in your report are reliable because you found great sources!

reliable sources of information. Sites like Wikipedia may be helpful. Its articles can be written and changed by anyone, though, so the information cannot always be counted on.

GIANT PANDA FACT AND OPINION CHART

Fact	Opinion
• Black and white fur	• Cute
• Up to 5 feet (1.5 m) long	• Everybody loves them
• Eat a lot of bamboo	• They love the taste of bamboo

Let's say you are doing a project on giant pandas. This comparison chart shows some facts and some opinions about pandas. Opinions are ideas that cannot be tested or proved.

WHAT DID YOU LEARN?

Once you have found the facts you need, what do you do with them? Simply listing what you have learned will not make for a very good project.

Think about what you have learned from your different sources. How do the facts fit together? How does one piece of information help you understand another? Does a fact you have learned

Once you have found sources on a topic, your job is not finished. You must read, decide which facts you want to use, and integrate, or put together, the ideas from all your sources and make them your own.

from one source **contradict** what you have learned from another? Which seems more accurate, and why?

What are the main ideas you have gained from your research, and what are the details that support these ideas? You might find it helpful to list

QUICK TIP

When you look closely at information and ask questions about it, you are thinking critically. Critical thinking is a skill you can use long after you turn in your report on Benjamin Franklin!

Taking notes about the information you find helps your brain organize and remember what you have learned. Do not forget to write down the sources for your facts. It will make it easier to find those sources again later if you need them.

CONCEPT WEB: REASONS FOR WESTWARD EXPANSION

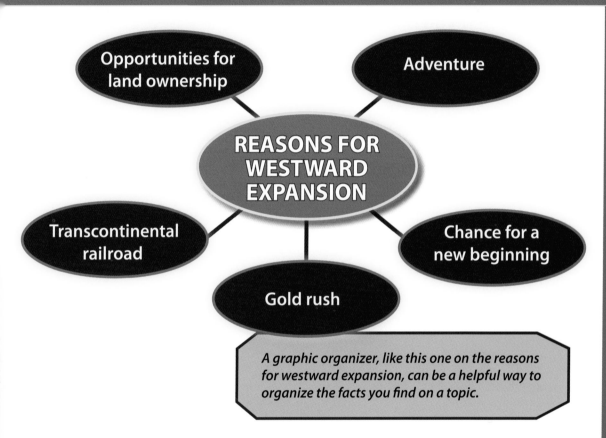

Opportunities for land ownership

Adventure

REASONS FOR WESTWARD EXPANSION

Transcontinental railroad

Chance for a new beginning

Gold rush

A graphic organizer, like this one on the reasons for westward expansion, can be a helpful way to organize the facts you find on a topic.

these ideas and details in a **graphic organizer** in order to see better what pieces fit together.

Remember that one of the most important points of a research project is to draw your own conclusions. If you are doing a research project on Frederick Douglass, think about what the facts of his life tell you about the times in which he lived.

GET CREATIVE!

When you do research, you are like a detective conducting an investigation. Libraries and the Internet are great sources of clues, but you should think about other ways to find information.

Asking experts directly can be a great way to find answers to your questions. If you want to find out

If you are working on a project about coral reefs, a visit to an aquarium could be a fun way to jump-start your research. Many aquariums hold talks at which you can hear an expert talk about a subject and ask questions, too.

What if you have an art project in which you have to make a piece of art in the style of a well-known artist, such as Monet? A visit to an art museum or the museum's website may be just the inspiration you need!

about dinosaurs, you could contact a paleontologist at your local natural-history museum. If you are writing a report about sea lions, visit an aquarium or zoo. You might even find experts in your own family, such as a grandfather who can tell you what it was like to fight in the Korean War. Just be sure to write down whom you spoke to and when.

Information is everywhere. It might not be possible to find every single fact there is about your topic. If you are creative and thorough in your research, though, you will learn a lot.

Sometimes you can find interesting information on a topic if you think creatively about keywords you can type into a search engine or database.

Glossary

access (AK-ses) To get something easily.

almanacs (AHL-muh-naks) Books with useful information, including information about the weather, and humorous stories.

contradict (kon-truh-DIKT) To say the opposite of, disagree, or have a different opinion.

details (dih-TAYLZ) Extra facts.

download (DOWN-lohd) To copy data from one computer system to another or to a disk.

foundation (fown-DAY-shun) The part on which other parts are built.

graphic organizer (GRA-fik OR-guh-ny-zer) A chart, graph, or picture that sorts facts and ideas and makes them clear.

institutions (in-stuh-TOO-shunz) Organizations founded for educational, religious, social, or other purposes.

observations (ahb-ser-VAY-shunz) Things that are seen or noticed.

periodicals (pir-ee-O-dih-kulz) News or information sources published at regular intervals.

statistics (stuh-TIS-tiks) Facts in the form of numbers.

subscription (sub-SKRIP-shun) An agreement to receive and to pay for something.

Index

Websites

Due to the changing nature of Internet links, PowerKids Press has developed an online list of websites related to the subject of this book. This site is updated regularly. Please use this link to access the list:

www.powerkidslinks.com/cs/find/